Perfect, Just Like You!™

By K.A. Wright

Illustrated by Starvos Pierce

perfectjustlikeyou.com
k.a.wright@perfectjustlikeyou.com
facebook.com/perfectjustlikeyou
@perfectjustlikeyou2018
@kawright15829091

It is with specific intent that this book elicits change and positively touches the ears, eyes ,minds, and hearts of everyone who comes into contact with it. May your hearts be opened and minds remain free. I believe these words to be true and they shall be granted unto me…..

To Larrilon with love! You will do great things in life. Take your time and believe in yourself every step of the way. You are a beautiful creative and I cant wait until you blossom into the beautiful being you were created to be. You deserve the world! Let the universe be your playground! I love You.

To my gorgeous mother Morlon, thank you for being in my corner and forever showering me with your unconditional love and always giving me that extra boost to keep going. I love you!

To my beautiful grandmother Juanita, thank you for encouraging me to go after what I want. It is because of you I chose to tap deeper into myself and follow my dreams.

To my father Kenneth! I did it! I appreciate you. I love you!

To Nancy and the Buschwick Babes, thank you for all that you have done for me. You are all awesome. I love you.

To Kris, thanks for all of your encouraging words and for keeping me on my toes! I love you.

To Leroy, thank you for everything. I appreciate you.

To Gerald and Minnie, thank you for speaking positivity over my life and being a listening ear.

To my aunts, I simply want to thank you beautiful ladies for always rooting for me and supporting my dreams. I appreciate you all more than you know. It's going to be a coin toss between all of you for who receives the first copy.

To my uncles, I appreciate you all for always being great examples of men and gifting me with your wisdom.

To Khadijah, thank you for always showing your love and support. I appreciate you. You're a trooper.

To my nieces, nephews, and cousins, I love you! All of you have your own personalities and I wish you all much success and health.

To my seeds, At this time you aren't here but if you ever get the opportunity to read this, I want you to know that everything that I have done and will continue to do has been accomplished with you in mind. It is my wish that you become the best version of yourselves. I love you.

To my friends and everyone else who has played a part in my life during this time, thank you for believing in my dreams and being patient with me. Thank your for your donations, your time and energy. I know at times it was rough, but you hung in there. For you I am grateful.

Love Stronger. Embrace Change. Remain Powerful. Become Your Best Self. Shine Your Light. Aim High. Create Balance.
TM

Standing in love, this book was written to encourage and memorialize the countless number of young children hurt and damaged by today's plague of low self esteem, bullying, and self hate. In an attempt to assist with changing the dynamics of how one may respond internally to the lasting effects of negative words and thoughts, I humbly present, *Perfect, Just Like You!*

It is my most sincere intention to uplift and encourage you to keep fighting your best fight when faced with adversity. May you find peace, power, and beauty, not only within the confines of this book, but deep within the most intimate parts of yourselves. Remember, it is okay to be different. Self acceptance is key. You are loved.

In the beginning of this story, there is you!
There is no one on Earth who is exactly like you!
No one can take your place.
You are your own individual.
You cannot be replaced.
Cuddly wuddly, super-duper cute,
You are who you are,
And everything is perfect, just like you!

You are beautiful and unique!
Checkout those teeth.
They are all shiny and clean.
One of the prettiest smiles
I've seen in a while.
Cuddly wuddly, super-duper cute,
Your teeth are your teeth,
And they are perfect, just like you!

Psst. Come here.
Aren't you happy that you can feel and/or hear?
I would love to tickle those cute little ears.
Cuddly wuddly, super-duper cute,
Your ears are your ears,
And they are perfect, just like you!

Oh my! Look at your amazing hair!
Everyone stops to stare!
Your crown looks marvelous up there!
Accept it and all of its glory.
You are beautiful with or without it in this story.
Cuddly wuddly, super-duper cute,
Your hair is your hair,
And it is perfect, just like you!

Your healthy and radiant skin is magnificent!
You have been kissed by the sun. Embrace it!
Never think about trading it with anyone!
Cuddly wuddly, super-duper cute,
Your skin is your skin,
And it is perfect, just like you!

What a surprise! Those stunning eyes
That twinkle just like the stars.
No matter the shade, make no mistake,
They have a funny way of showing people
Who you really are.
Cuddly wuddly, super-duper cute,
Your eyes are your eyes,
And they are perfect, just like you!

Wow! There it goes! Sitting in the perfect place,
Right in the center of your perfect face,
We call it a nose!
Cuddly wuddly, super-duper cute,
Your nose is your nose,
And it is perfect, just like you!

Let me see those wonderful hands.
Wiggle them as fast as you can!
They were made to receive,
And give help to anyone in time of need.
When it's hot, they can be used as fans.
Cuddly wuddly, super-duper cute,
Your hands are your hands,
And they are perfect, just like you!

You are absolutely amazing and sweet,
But I must warn you to cherish your feet and to
Take extra care of your toes.
Those little critters get you where you need to go.
They are always the right size, whatever shoe fits,
Give them a try. When they are not clean,
The stinky smell tickles the nose.
Cuddly wuddly, super-duper cute,
Your feet are your feet,
And they are perfect, just like you!

Having a disability or disease
Doesn't mean that you're weak.
You are beyond strong. It is a super power indeed.
Whether you have crutches or a wheeled chair,
Just remember that
You are a beautiful, blossoming flower
With tons of love to share.
Cuddly wuddly, super-duper cute,
Your superpower is your superpower,
And it is perfect, just like you!

Short or tall, big or small, height doesn't matter.
Having a big heart is what counts!
You are loved just the same.
You may not be tall as a tree, or bigger than me,
But you are exactly as tall or small
As you were designed to be.
Cuddly wuddly, super-duper cute,
Your height is your height,
And it is perfect, just like you!

You are bold and confident!
Don't let people fill your mind with chatter.
They can say whatever they want about your body.
Just remember that size doesn't matter.
Cuddly wuddly, super-duper cute,
Your body is your body,
And it is perfect, just like you!

ITY
NEGATIV
NEG
NEG
ATIV
ITY

Who are you?
Do not be ashamed.
It is an incredible claim to carry your name.
Your parents gave it to for a reason.
It is your power.
It is your peace.
Say it with authority.
Find its meaning and live accordingly.
Cuddly wuddly, super-duper cute,
Your name is your name,
And it is perfect, just like you!

Hello
My name is

In the end of this story, there is still you!
There is still no one on Earth who is exactly like you!
No one can take your place.
You are your own individual.
You cannot be replaced.
Cuddly wuddly, super-duper cute,
You are who you are,
And everything is perfect, just like you!

Your
Picture
Here
PERFECT

AFFIRMATIONS:

I AM BEAUTIFUL
I AM SMART
I AM AN INTRICATE PIECE OF ART
I AM HEALTHY
I AM UNIQUE
FROM MY HEAD TO MY FEET
I AM AS PERFECT AS PERFECT CAN BE

Smart
Healthy
I am
Beautiful
Unique
Perfect
29

If someone says something to you or touches you in a way that hurts you or makes you feel uncomfortable, please let a grown up know. DO NOT KEEP QUIET. We understand that you may be scared. You did nothing wrong. Your body is your sacred instrument and no one has the right to touch it without your permission. You are loved.

Meet the Crew

K.A. Wright is a massage therapist, actor, performing artist, and now a first time author of his debut children's books, "Perfect, Just Like You!" and its companion, "Perfect Just Like You Coloring Book/Workbook!" "Perfect, Just Like You!" uses beautiful rhythmic poems to tackle low self-esteem, bullying, and self-hate with the intent of restoring confidence within children around the world while its companion uses a therapeutic approach by allowing children to freely express themselves and add color to their world as they see fit.

He was inspired to write "Perfect, Just Like You!" when he learned his five year old cousin expressed discontent for dolls that looked like her. Recognizing that her reaction reflected the development of a harmful self-image, Wright wanted to write something that could help his cousin and other children understand the importance of self-love.

Wright is fascinated by the stories and modes of self-expression of others. As a middle child who has been both the admiring younger sibling and protective older brother, he understands the importance of discovering and sharing one's voice. Wright has been expressing himself through poetry since middle school and later extended that self-expression through the crafts of massage therapy, acting, and performing arts. He believes that all art is life and it can be used as a vehicle to nurture the world in which we live and upon which we all have a great responsibility to make a positive impact.

To stay connected with K. A. Wright and future projects, please subscribe to the email list and also like, share, and follow him on all social media platforms. Thank you for your support! Have a Cuddly Wuddly Day!!!

- perfectjustlikeyou.com
- k.a.wright@perfectjustlikeyou.com
- facebook.com/perfectjustlikeyou
- @perfectjustlikeyou2018
- @kawright15829091

CPSIA information can be obtained at www.ICGtesting.com
Printed in the USA
LVIW011645210620
658644LV00007B/21